THE UNKNOWN SOLDIER

LINDA GRANFIELD

NORTH WINDS PRESS
AN IMPRINT OF SCHOLASTIC CANADA LTD.

In memory of those men and women of the world's armed forces
who rest unknown in graves, marked and unmarked,
on the land and beneath the sea.

Library and Archives Canada Cataloguing in Publication
Granfield, Linda
The unknown soldier / Linda Granfield.

ISBN 978-0-439-93558-6

1. War memorials--Juvenile literature. 2. Soldiers' monuments--Juvenile
literature. 3. Unknown military personnel--Juvenile literature. I. Title.
NA9325.G72 2008   j355.1'6   C2008-900895-2

ISBN 10 0-439-93558-X

6 5 4 3 2   Printed in Singapore 46   12 13 14 15

UNKNOWN

Young faces, fresh-scrubbed and eager,
once dressed in farm or company clothes,
now clad in a nation's, *their* nation's, uniform.

Once embraced by loving arms,
chucked under the chin,
rocked with joy.
Young men ready to please, ready to serve,
still ready to play and to love.

Now embraced by the earth and marble,
or in a watery grave unmarked,
or in no grave at all.

Embraced by history.
Remembered,
and still —

Unknown

— *Linda Granfield*

TABLE OF CONTENTS

War, Peace and . . . After 3

Canada 6

France 10

Britain 12

The United States 14

Tributes, Traditions and Tales 16

Italy 18

Belgium 19

Poland 20

Germany 21

Greece 22

Japan 23

Russia 24

Iraq 25

Australia 26

New Zealand 27

And Elsewhere 28

Unknown — No Longer 29

Symbols Often Seen on Tombs and Gravestones 32

Significant Events 34

Lest We Forget 35

Glossary 36

Acknowledgements/Credits 37

Index 38

WAR, PEACE AND . . . AFTER

BY THE TIME the First World War ended in 1918, millions of young men in the armed forces, as well as more millions of civilians, were dead. For four long years, the battles of what was called the Great War had devastated entire countries. Bombarded villages had disappeared. Farm fields that had once supplied life-giving grains and produce had become bloody and muddy final resting places.

On Armistice Day, at the 11th hour of the 11th day of the 11th month, 1918, the war ended. It was time to begin rebuilding ruined cities and to create new partnerships between countries. Those who had survived the horrible battles of the Great War could look forward to returning to their homes, to once again feel the warm embrace of a parent, wife or much-grown child. However, the happiness and family celebrations brought by the end of war were balanced in equal measure by the grief and loneliness felt when loved ones never returned. Where were they?

A photo showing one soldier tending another's grave might bring the families back home some bit of comfort, but grave maintenance was not always possible during wartime.

Many of the Great War's dead had been hastily buried near where they fell. Wooden crosses, painted with the soldiers' names, provided temporary markers, put in place as the remaining soldiers moved on. Sometimes a dead soldier's injuries were so severe no one knew the identity of the person being buried, or the explosions were so fierce there was nothing left to bury. Sometimes many bodies were buried in one mass grave. Sometimes battles at sea resulted in watery graves for nearly all on board. And sometimes previously known graves literally disappeared because of shelling later in the war.

After the war, the dead were reburied with dignity and care in new, permanent cemeteries. The wooden crosses were replaced by white marble stones etched with the soldiers' names. Unfortunately, not every one of the fallen could be identified for reburial. Harsh rains, snow and sun had erased many of the names on the wooden crosses. These new "unknowns" were to lie for eternity beneath stones that read: *A Soldier of the Great War — Known To God.*

During the Second World War (1939–1945) and the Korean War (1950–1953), a similar burial process was followed. The practice was once again to bury soldiers near where they had died in battle. New cemeteries were filled and detailed records kept.

After all the wars, many North American families travelled overseas, often at great expense, to visit a loved one's grave and have their photograph taken alongside it, as they might never be at that spot again. Pilgrimages were organized to take large groups from one country to the cemeteries of another.

Today, the burial of Canadians who die in times of war is handled much differently, thanks to new technologies. Helicopters often deliver the fallen to huge military planes that take them back home in a matter of

The crosses that were seen "row on row" in the early war cemeteries were sometimes made of scrap wood. Different styles were made, depending on the craftsmanship of the soldier making the marker.

hours. Families are able to bury their son or daughter in a family plot, or in a national cemetery in their land of birth.

The science of genetic identification means there will be far fewer "unknowns." But while this science has greatly changed, the emotions of new generations have not. We continue to honour and remember the soldiers we knew . . . and the millions we never could know.

Memorials, monuments and symbols such as the red poppy or a sprig of rosemary provide people around the world with a focus for remembrance.

Thousands of unknown soldiers' graves around the world read *Known To God/Known Unto God*. Red roses have been planted in many of the military cemeteries because poppies, which they represent, would engulf the graves if left to grow untended.

CANADA

The Tomb of the Unknown Soldier
Le Tombeau du Soldat Inconnu

BRINGING CANADA'S OWN unknown soldier home in 2000 was part of a long tradition that began in France during the Great War and gained momentum in the 1920s. Since that time, nations around the world have created tombs, arches and other monuments as lasting memorials to those soldiers "known to God."

As the new millennium drew near, the Royal Canadian Legion proposed that the remains of one of Canada's twenty-seven thousand unknown servicemen and women be repatriated for national commemoration.

In 1997, the Legion began working with other veterans' organizations and government ministries to establish a Tomb of the Unknown Soldier in Ottawa. The Tomb honours all Canadians, in any branch of the armed forces, "who died or may die for their country in all battles — past, present, and future."

The Commonwealth War Graves Commission selected an unidentified Canadian soldier who had fought in the Great War. This soldier had originally been buried in the Cabaret-Rouge British Cemetery in Souchez, France. On May 16, 2000, he was disinterred and placed in a casket made from the wood of a silver maple. After a brief ceremony at the Vimy Memorial, the casket was flown back to Canada.

The sword, helmet, laurel branch and maple leaves that lie on top of the Tomb are patterned after motifs on the altar of the Vimy Memorial. Artist Mary-Ann Liu created the winning design for the Tomb. While all of the competitors were given the same materials to consider, granite and bronze, Liu's version with polished and rough textures symbolizes a transformation from life to death.

The towering Vimy Memorial in France, designed by Canadian Walter Allward, was restored and rededicated in April 2007 for the ninetieth anniversary of the Battle of Vimy Ridge.

The selection of Vimy for the ceremony demonstrated its importance in Canada's history. The Battle of Vimy Ridge began at dawn on Easter Monday, April 9, 1917. Over the next few days, Canadian soldiers achieved a victory that other nations had been unable to accomplish. But the price was high: over three thousand Canadians were killed; more than seven thousand wounded. In 1936, a magnificent memorial, inscribed with the names of more than eleven thousand Canadians who died in France during the First World War and whose resting place is unknown, was built on part of the Vimy battlefield. The name of the Canadian unknown soldier, whoever he is, is carved on the Memorial.

Once the body was back home in Canada, thousands quietly paid their respects while the casket rested in the Peace Tower on Parliament Hill. On the morning of May 28, 2000, the casket was placed upon a gun carriage for its final journey to the base of the National War Memorial. The Unknown was buried in a Quebec granite sarcophagus in front of the Memorial at Ottawa's Confederation Square.

While thousands along the route applauded the Unknown, millions more across the country watched the proceedings on television.

Beneath the watchful eyes of bronze soldiers poised above him, Canada's unknown soldier was laid to rest. A piper, Royal Canadian Mounted Police and representatives of the armed forces were present.

Grand Chief Howard Anderson sprinkled a mixture of tobacco and sweetgrass on the casket — sacred plants that represent purification, respect and gratitude.

Earth from the Unknown's original grave in France, as well as from every Canadian province and territory, was poured on the casket. Grand Chief Howard Anderson placed a Golden Eagle feather (sometimes awarded to First Nations warriors who have been strong, brave and loyal) upon the samples of earth.

Paul Métivier, a hundred-year-old First World War veteran, and Ernest "Smokey" Smith, who won the Victoria Cross during the Second World War, read poet Laurence Binyon's words: *At the going down of the sun, and in the morning, we will remember them.*

The unknown soldier's original gravestone was placed in a small room specially built for it at the Canadian War Museum in Ottawa. Each year, at eleven o'clock on the morning of November 11, sunlight streams through the window and onto the gravestone.

ANCIENNE SEPULTURE D'UN
SOLDAT CANADIEN INCONNU
MORT AU COURS DE LA
PREMIERE GUERRE MONDIALE.
IL A ETE EXHUME
LE 25 MAI 2000
ET IL REPOSE MAINTENANT AU
MONUMENT COMMEMORATIF
DE GUERRE DU CANADA
A OTTAWA.

THE FORMER GRAVE OF AN
UNKNOWN CANADIAN SOLDIER
OF THE FIRST WORLD WAR.
HIS REMAINS WERE REMOVED
ON 25 MAY 2000 AND NOW
LIE INTERRED AT THE
NATIONAL WAR MEMORIAL
IN OTTAWA CANADA.

In France, a new marker was placed upon the original grave of the Canadian unknown soldier.

The Tomb lies beside the National War Memorial. In 2007, soldiers from the Governor General's honour guard began to serve as daytime ceremonial sentinels. During the changing of the guard, the soldiers vow to protect the Tomb during their watch.

A grandfather pauses to explain to his granddaughter why people pay their respects at the Tomb of the Unknown Soldier.

9

FRANCE

Le Tombeau du Soldat Inconnu

WHILE THE GREAT WAR was still being fought on her soil, France was considering honouring one soldier who would symbolize the many who had already fallen. By the end of the war, nearly one and a half million French soldiers had died, over four million were wounded, and France itself lay in ruins.

Shortly after the Armistice was signed in 1918, the government decided to proceed with its plans to honour an unidentified soldier. At first, the location selected for the burial was the Pantheon, a building in Paris where famous French citizens are buried. French veterans, however, preferred the Arc de Triomphe, a site that for almost one hundred years had been identified with military history.

But how to choose that one soldier? On

In 1806, French Emperor Napoleon Bonaparte (1769–1821) decreed that a triumphal arch be built to commemorate one of his military victories. Napoleon died before the Arc de Triomphe was completed in 1836.

Collection E. DESMAISONS

PARIS
L'Arc de Triomphe.

The Arc de Triomphe stands in Place Charles-de-Gaulle, a star-shaped intersection in Paris once known as Place de l'Etoile.

490 bis - Le Tombeau du Soldat Inconnu
inhumé sous l'Arc de Triomphe le 11 Nov. 1920
Tomb of the Unknown Soldier
intered under the Arch of Triumph
on the 11 Nov. 1920   A. P.

Dignitaries and relatives of French soldiers adorned the new Tomb with huge bouquets. The bronze palm plaques are tributes from towns and associations.

Click! During the Second World War, German troops who occupied Paris had souvenir photographs taken beneath the historic arch.

November 10, 1920, veteran Auguste Thin entered a torchlit room in Verdun's Citadel. In it were eight coffins containing unknown soldiers' remains. Thin walked around them all and then selected the sixth coffin — *this* was to be the one. On November 11, France's unknown soldier was brought to the Arc de Triomphe in Paris. In January 1921 he was moved from a room inside the Arc to a vault where he now rests. The stone slab that marks his grave reads: *Here rests a French soldier who died for his country.* Grateful citizens, believing that this Unknown might be a family member, piled flowers high and wept.

Across the English Channel, on that same November day, another ceremony had begun.

An eternal flame (Flame of Remembrance) was first lit on November 11, 1923. It is symbolically relit every evening at 6:30. On his first day in office in May 2007, French president Nicolas Sarkozy placed a wreath at the Tomb and relit the flame, which now represents the fallen of both world wars.

11

BRITAIN
The Tomb of the Unknown Warrior

ON THE SAME DAY that the French were burying their Unknown, black-coated Londoners were silently crowding the streets and craning their necks to view the gun carriage that bore their unknown warrior to his final resting place in Westminster Abbey. Children sat upon adults' shoulders to better see King George V and the procession. Far from the chaos of the Great War battlefields, veterans stood in solemn rows, remembering.

The idea of a grave for an unknown British soldier was originally brought to the government's attention by the Reverend David Railton, who had served as a chaplain during the Great War. In 1920, the Dean of Westminster supported Railton's idea and the government agreed that one burial could symbolize those of thousands of British soldiers with no known grave.

Westminster Abbey, established in 1065, has been the site of nearly every coronation of a British king or queen since 1066. The Houses of Parliament can be seen behind the Abbey.

London.

Westminster Abbey.

The warrior's cortège arrived at the Cenotaph (designed by Sir Edwin Lutyens) just before the famous bell Big Ben tolled the first stroke of eleven. Two minutes of silence followed. Then King George V proceeded with the cortège to the Abbey.

GRAPHIC PHOTO UNION. FUNERAL OF 'THE 'UNKNOWN WARRIOR'. 162.S. BEAGLES' POSTCARDS. THE COFFIN PASSING THE CENOTAPH MEMORIAL

A black marble slab later replaced the temporary marker. The words on it include these: They buried him among the kings, because he had done good toward God and toward His house.

One hundred representatives of the armed forces, many wearing the Victoria Cross (the highest British award for gallantry in action) attended the burial. An honour guard stood watch for seven days while more than a million mourners paid their last respects.

On November 18, 1920, a temporary stone sealed the grave. *Greater Love Hath No Man Than This* was etched upon it.

On November 7, 1920, the bodies of British soldiers from four major battlefields were wrapped with the Union Jack and placed in the chapel at St. Pol, France. At midnight, Brigadier-General L.J. Wyatt selected one body as the unknown warrior. The other Unknowns were reburied.

The Unknown's simple coffin was escorted to the city of Boulogne-sur-Mer and placed inside a casket made of oak from the royal estate at Hampton Court. A sixteenth-century Crusader's sword was placed on top. The French troops paid their last respects before a ship transported the Unknown to England.

On November 11, the unknown warrior was laid to rest in a tomb lined with soil from Ypres, France. He remains in Westminster Abbey, with many of Britain's most honoured dead.

THE UNITED STATES

The Tomb of the Unknowns

EARLY IN 1921, the United States Congress approved plans for the burial of an unidentified American soldier in the plaza of the Memorial Amphitheater in Arlington National Cemetery, the most renowned burial place for men and women who served in the United States armed forces.

By November 11, 1921, America's unknown soldier had travelled from France to Washington. National newspapers filled pages with stories about those who came to the Capitol hoping this soldier might be a missing member of their family.

The *Springfield Daily Republican* said:
Many persons in the public line carried floral offerings of their own on which there seldom was a card. In nearly every instance these voluntary offerings were carried by a child. . . . old men and old women, the grandparents of some soldier, perhaps, were the most visibly affected, tears streaming down their cheeks as they turned around for a farewell look at the flower-covered coffin.

Sergeant Edward F. Younger selected America's first unknown soldier. He was given a bouquet of roses and left alone with four unmarked caskets. Younger placed the flowers on one casket and saluted. The bouquet was buried along with the unknown soldier. The remaining soldiers were buried in the Meuse-Argonne American Cemetery in France.

The USS *Olympia*, bearing the casket, sailed from Le Havre, France, to Washington, D.C. This stereoscope card entitled "Back to Home Land!" shows the casket piped ashore and met by dignitaries, among them American General John Pershing, standing on the rainy dock.

14

On November 10, 1921, a visitor took this spectacular snapshot of the Capitol. She, like nearly a hundred thousand others, filed past the unknown soldier's casket as it lay in state until midnight. *The night the unknown soldier lay under the dome* is her caption.

Tomb of Unknown Soldier. Arlington National Cemetery.

The first Tomb of the Unknown Soldier was a very simple marble base and plinth. In 1926, Congress authorized funds for further completion of the Tomb and invited American architects to submit designs. Construction of the present tomb began in 1931.

The Unknown made his last journey by gun carriage, and was buried overlooking his nation's capital. Beneath his casket lay soil brought from the French battlefields where he had fought, died and was first buried.

On Memorial Day, May 30, 1958, two other unknown soldiers from the Second World War and the Korean War were also buried there. The name of the tomb was changed to the Tomb of the Unknowns. In 1984, a fourth soldier, from the Vietnam War, joined his fellow soldiers. The identity of the Vietnam Unknown was later disputed.

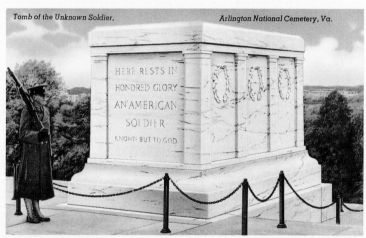

Tomb of the Unknown Soldier,   Arlington National Cemetery, Va.

HERE RESTS IN HONORED GLORY AN AMERICAN SOLDIER KNOWN BUT TO GOD

The finished marble sarcophagus was opened to the public in April 1932. The front of the Tomb shows the female figures of Victory and Peace and a male figure representing Valour. On the rear panel are the words: *Here Rests in Honored Glory An American Soldier Known But To God.*

At the burial, Aleek-chea-ahoosh/ Plenty Coups, chief of the Apsáalooke/Crow people, honoured a fellow warrior as he removed his eagle-feather headdress and placed it and his coup stick upon the casket.

The Tomb and guard (left) during Memorial Day ceremonies.

15

TRIBUTES, TRADITIONS AND TALES

SINCE 1920, when the first national tomb of an unknown soldier was established, the themes of peace and the unknown soldier have been associated with *all* who served, and have inspired tributes of remembrance.

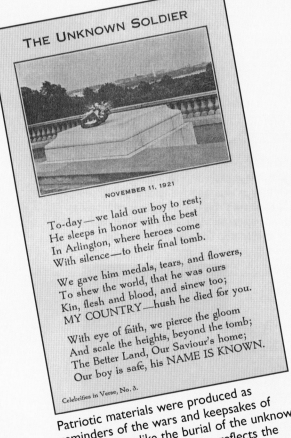

THE UNKNOWN SOLDIER

NOVEMBER 11, 1921

To-day—we laid our boy to rest;
He sleeps in honor with the best
In Arlington, where heroes come
With silence—to their final tomb.

We gave him medals, tears, and flowers,
To shew the world, that he was ours
Kin, flesh and blood, and sinew too;
MY COUNTRY—hush he died for you.

With eye of faith, we pierce the gloom
And scale the heights, beyond the tomb;
The Better Land, Our Saviour's home;
Our boy is safe, his NAME IS KNOWN.

Celebrities in Verse, No. 3.

Patriotic materials were produced as reminders of the wars and keepsakes of special events, like the burial of the unknown soldier. This postcard's poem reflects the gratitude of a nation.

Mary Raymond Shipman Andrews's short novel *Yellow Butterflies* was based on newspaper articles documenting the burial of the American unknown soldier. The image of the yellow Cloudless Sulphur butterfly came to symbolize the immortality of the selected soldier.

Every Canadian Remembrance Day since 2000, at the end of the national ceremonies in Ottawa, people have left their poppy pins on the Tomb.

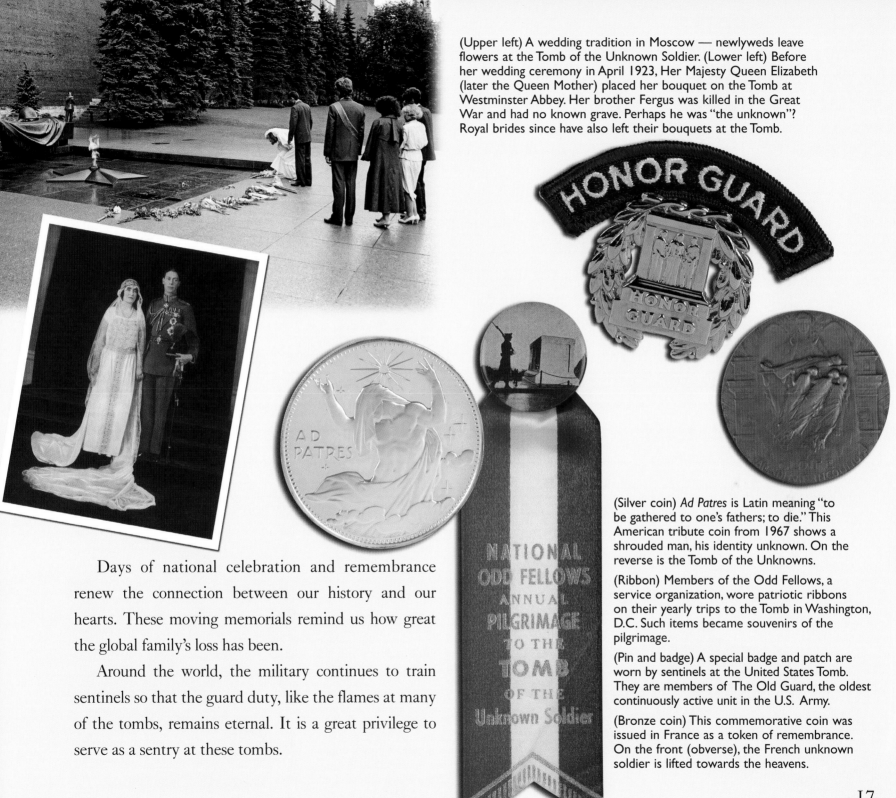

(Upper left) A wedding tradition in Moscow — newlyweds leave flowers at the Tomb of the Unknown Soldier. (Lower left) Before her wedding ceremony in April 1923, Her Majesty Queen Elizabeth (later the Queen Mother) placed her bouquet on the Tomb at Westminster Abbey. Her brother Fergus was killed in the Great War and had no known grave. Perhaps he was "the unknown"? Royal brides since have also left their bouquets at the Tomb.

Days of national celebration and remembrance renew the connection between our history and our hearts. These moving memorials remind us how great the global family's loss has been.

Around the world, the military continues to train sentinels so that the guard duty, like the flames at many of the tombs, remains eternal. It is a great privilege to serve as a sentry at these tombs.

(Silver coin) *Ad Patres* is Latin meaning "to be gathered to one's fathers; to die." This American tribute coin from 1967 shows a shrouded man, his identity unknown. On the reverse is the Tomb of the Unknowns.

(Ribbon) Members of the Odd Fellows, a service organization, wore patriotic ribbons on their yearly trips to the Tomb in Washington, D.C. Such items became souvenirs of the pilgrimage.

(Pin and badge) A special badge and patch are worn by sentinels at the United States Tomb. They are members of The Old Guard, the oldest continuously active unit in the U.S. Army.

(Bronze coin) This commemorative coin was issued in France as a token of remembrance. On the front (obverse), the French unknown soldier is lifted towards the heavens.

17

ITALY
La tomba del Milite Ignoto

A train carried the unknown soldier to Rome. Along the route, Italians tossed flowers onto the casket and outdoor masses were celebrated. "The mothers of the fallen" watched the unknown soldier pass by.

ITALY, A NEUTRAL COUNTRY when the Great War broke out in 1914, joined the Allies in 1915. In the summer of 1921, officials decided that an unknown soldier, one of the nearly six hundred thousand Italian soldiers who died in the First World War, would be buried in Rome with all possible honours. The ceremony would take place on November 4, Victory Day (now known as National Unity Day). There was much to be done and little time to prepare, but with great passion and patriotism, a unified nation buried one special son and mourned all of its fallen on the appointed day.

Maria Bergamas, a woman from Trieste who had lost her son Antonio in the war, was asked to select one of eleven coffins. She reportedly dropped her black veil upon her choice. The other caskets were buried in the Cemetery of the Heroes in Aquileia. Bergamas was also buried there in 1954.

Il Vittoriano, where the Unknown is buried, was built to honour Victor Emmanuel II, the first king of a unified Italy.

Two guards watch over *Il Milite Ignoto*. An eternal flame burns nearby. The casket of the Unknown was placed into a shelf-like crypt at the feet of the goddess Roma, the city's protector.

BELGIUM

het graf van de Onbekende Soldaat
Le Tombeau du Soldat Inconnu

ON NOVEMBER 10, 1922, in dim flickering torch-light, the remains of five unknown soldiers, taken from five major Belgian battlefields, were placed in a semicircle in the railway station at Bruges. The dimness, however, did not hinder Raymond Haesebrouck, the local man who had been asked to select Belgium's unknown soldier. Haesebrouck had been blinded in the Great War, yet he moved directly to the fourth casket — this soldier would be the one.

Immense lions, representing courage and bravery, protect the grave. Belgian soldiers who died in the Second World War are remembered on a second engraved flagstone at the Tomb.

On November 11, 1922, before the royal family and veterans of the Great War, Belgium's unknown soldier was buried in a crypt in front of the Column. Years later, in 2007, government officials stood at the Column to honour over two hundred Belgians who had died in peace missions abroad since 1945 — among them ten soldiers killed during the 1994 civil war in Rwanda and mourned around the world.

The Congress Column in Brussels was completed in 1859 to commemorate the Congress of 1830 that resulted in the writing of the Belgian Constitution. (Inset) Some profits from souvenir postcards were used to support *les orphelins de la guerre* (war orphans).

19

POLAND

Grób Nieznanego Żolnierza

A STONE MARKER to honour the fallen soldiers of both the Great War and the Polish-Soviet War (1919–1920) already stood near Warsaw's magnificent Saxon Palace *(Palac Saski)*, but a more significant tribute was to come.

In 1925, officials said they wanted to include an Unknown from the 1918 Battle of Lwów (now Lviv in Ukraine). That October, three coffins were exhumed from Łyczakowski Cemetery. The mother of Konstanty Zarugiewicz, a teenaged sol-

dier who had died in 1920 and never been located, was asked to select the Unknown.

After services in Warsaw's St. John's Cathedral, the unknown soldier was buried beneath the floor of the graceful colonnade that joined the two wings of the palace. But the Second World War brought destruction to Poland, and the columns crowning the colonnade were broken — symbols of life cut short, just as Konstanty's had been.

In 1944, the Saxon Palace was destroyed by the occupying German army. Only the sheltering arches and the Tomb inside were left standing. After the war, the rubble was removed and the building made safe for visitors.

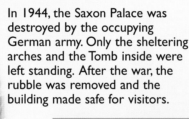

Gouges on the column (at left) recall the damage done in 1944. Guards remain on watch, as they have since 1925, except during the German occupation. Every hour a changing of the guard occurs.

The Tomb is located near the beautiful Saxon Garden, which has delighted the public since 1727. The huge palace is being rebuilt and the Tomb will be a part of it once again.

GERMANY

Zentrale Gedenkstätte der Bundesrepublick Deutschland

AFTER THE GREAT WAR, Berlin's *Neue Wache* (New Guardhouse) was redesigned to become a place of remembrance: the Memorial for the Fallen of the World War. Inside the building stood a huge block of black stone topped by a wreath of silver and gold oak leaves. A circular hole (oculus) in the roof let in light, rain and snow.

During the Second World War, the building was damaged by bombs, the wreath stolen. Another restoration in 1962 included yet another name and purpose: the Memorial to the Victims of Fascism and Militarism.

An eternal flame once glowed inside a glass box at the Memorial. Beneath the floor, two urns held the remains of an unknown concentration-camp inmate and the remains of an unknown German soldier from the Second World War. The urns' whereabouts are no longer known.

In 1969, the German Democratic Republic buried two Unknowns beneath the floor and added an eternal flame. Honour guards once again marched outside. When East and West Germany unified in 1990, the memorial was closed and the eternal flame was removed.

Since 1993, the building has been called the Central Memorial of the Federal Republic of Germany for the Victims of War and Tyranny.

Neue Wache as it appeared one hundred years ago. The building's exterior looks the same today.

An enlarged version of a sculpture by Käthe Kollwitz is the focal point of the Memorial. Kollwitz lost both her son and grandson, one in each world war.

21

GREECE

Το Μνημείο του Αγνώστου Στρατιώτη

IN ANCIENT ATHENS, GREECE, a public funeral was held for the Athenians who had died in 430 BCE, the first year of the Peloponnesian War. An empty coffin, representing those soldiers whose bodies were never recovered, was decorated and carried with honour to the burial place.

Pericles, a famous statesman and orator, began his funeral oration during the burial. Quotations from his speech can be seen over two thousand years later, carved into the walls of the Tomb of the Unknown Soldier in Athens. The memorial is built below the pale yellow Parliament Building, facing Syntagma (Constitution) Square.

In 1925, the Greek government decided that it, like other nations around the world, would honour those who died in the Great War. A design competition was won in 1926 by Emmanuel Lazaridis, but the monument was not completed and dedicated until Independence Day, March 25, 1932.

According to the customs of the ancient Greek peoples, the Tomb remains empty. It is a symbolic resting place for all Greek unknown soldiers.

A carved relief of a fallen soldier of ancient Greece, wearing his plumed helmet and holding his shield, is the central image at the Tomb. The floral tributes and soldiers suggest that this photo was taken when the Tomb was dedicated in 1932.

ΑΘΗΝΑΙ. Ὁ Τάφος τοῦ Ἀφανοῦς Στρατιώτου.
ATHÈNES. La Tombe du Soldat inconnu.

Quotations, carved near the relief, say that a vacant coffin was brought for the unknown heroes, and that "every land is the tomb of the heroes." The names of battles where Greeks fought, as well as bronze shields, honour the fallen.

Official guards, called *evzones*, are on duty. Like other Tomb guards around the world, they are part of an elite corps intent on doing their job well and with great respect.

JAPAN

千鳥ヶ淵　戦没者墓苑

IN 1953, THE JAPANESE CABINET established Chidorigafuchi National Cemetery, near the Imperial Palace in Tokyo, to honour the dead of the Second World War. Japanese soldiers' remains from foreign battlefields were buried here. In 1959, a pavilion was built as a symbolic resting place for the Unknown.

In May 2005, the ashes of more than three hundred Japanese unknown soldiers were added to those already in the Tomb of Unknown Soldiers. Dignitaries and a member of Japan's royal family each placed a chrysanthemum on a table near the casket and urn containing the ashes. There are no guards or eternal flames at the quiet Tomb.

At nearby Yasukuni Shrine, Japan's two and a half million known war dead are honoured. Debate about the Shrine erupted in 1978, when it was learned that the spirits of the war dead enshrined there included names of convicted war criminals from the Second World War. The controversy has still not been resolved.

Each spring, the fragile cherry blossoms of Chidorigafuchi bring tourists from around the world.

The chrysanthemum is the floral emblem of Japan. It also represents the Imperial Family. The chrysanthemum's petals are believed to represent the sun (life) and perfection. White chrysanthemums, symbolic of mourning in Japan, are often placed on graves there.

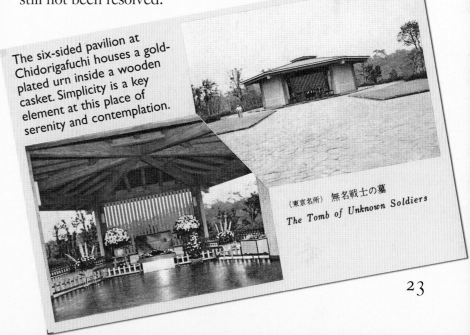

The six-sided pavilion at Chidorigafuchi houses a gold-plated urn inside a wooden casket. Simplicity is a key element at this place of serenity and contemplation.

（東京名所）　無名戦士の墓
The Tomb of Unknown Soldiers

23

RUSSIA

Могила Неизвестного Солдата

EVERY MAY, ON VICTORY DAY, the president of the Russian Federation lays a wreath at the Tomb of the Unknown Soldier outside the Kremlin walls in Moscow. Veterans of the Great Patriotic War (the Second World War) attend the ceremonies. Victory Day celebrates the German surrender to the then-Soviet Union and her allies on May 8, 1945.

The beautiful Alexandrovsky Gardens outside the Kremlin's west wall were selected as the site for the Tomb. In December 1966, the body of an unknown soldier was brought to Moscow from the village of Kryukovo, the closest the German army came to Russia's capital during the war.

The Tomb was unveiled on May 8, 1967. The words *Your Name is Unknown, Your Deeds are Immortal* are inscribed on the polished black stone floor, near the eternal flame. On Victory Day, all of Russia observes a moment of silence to honour the nation's fallen — among them, the Unknown.

The bronze helmet, laurel and military standard were added to the Tomb in 1975. A nearby wall bears the words: *1941– In Memory of Those Who Died for the Motherland – 1945.* The eternal flame was brought to Moscow from St. Petersburg.

Russia's unknown soldier is buried near the Corner Arsenal Tower, built in 1492. The colossal brick wall of the Kremlin ("the fortress") overlooks the Tomb.

The guards, called Number One Post, were stationed at revolutionary leader Nikolai (Vladimir) Lenin's tomb in nearby Red Square from 1924 until 1993. In 1997, the Post was assigned a new task, protecting the grave of the unknown soldier.

IRAQ
نصب الجندي المجهول

IN BAGHDAD, near gurgling fountains, a huge copper *dira'a* (shield) looks as though it has just been dropped by a falling soldier. Red granite and white marble, stained glass and stainless steel are some of the many materials used to build Iraq's Monument to the Unknown Soldier. A white sculpture under the *dira'a* represents the spirit of the Unknown being released.

Former president Saddam Hussein decreed that a monument be constructed to honour an unknown soldier from the Iran-Iraq War. This Tomb, opened in 1982, has been the subject of controversy. Is it a tribute to Iraq's unknown dead, or a monument to honour the leader who declared war?

Committees continue to debate whether the Tomb and other monuments erected by Hussein should be destroyed because of the regime they represent, or kept as reminders of a crucial period in the country's history. The Tomb, which had been damaged by bombing during the second Gulf War, was repaired, and the restored Monument unveiled to the public on Iraqi Army Day in January 2006.

The new Monument to the Unknown Soldier appeared on the old Iraqi five-*dinar* and ten-thousand-*dinar* notes.

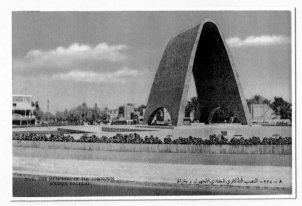

Iraq's original Unknown Soldier Monument was built in 1959 in Baghdad's Firdos Square. The Monument itself was demolished in 1982 and later replaced with a statue of Hussein. The toppling of the statue in 2003 during the second Gulf War was televised around the world.

The enormous Monument covers an area the size of many football fields. The stained-glass spiral tower is a replica of the famous minaret in Samarra, Iraq, built over a thousand years ago by Caliph al-Mutawakil.

25

AUSTRALIA

The Tomb of the Unknown Australian Soldier

IN 1916, AUSTRALIAN war correspondent Charles Bean and archivist John Treloar dreamed of a building that would honour their country's Great War soldiers. In 1941, the Australian War Memorial opened; it became the resting place of the Australian unknown soldier over half a century later. On November 2, 1993, the remains of an Australian Unknown were removed from a French cemetery and transported to Canberra, Australia. In the Old Parliament House he lay in state in a coffin made of Tasmanian blackwood. A slouch hat, a sprig of yellow wattle (the national flower) and soil from a French battlefield were placed in the coffin with him.

The Unknown was lowered into the floor of the Hall of Memory at the Australian War Memorial on November 11, 1993. For three days, thousands of people passed the open crypt. Then it was sealed with a red Turkish marble slab inscribed with the words *An Unknown Australian Soldier Killed in the War of 1914–1918.*

The Hall of Memory (right) was added to the Australian War Memorial (above) in 1959, as a place of contemplation. With the addition of the Tomb in 1993, the Memorial is now also a national shrine. The Hall's mosaic walls depict a soldier, seaman, airman and servicewoman. The four pillars represent the four ancient elements: air, earth, fire and water.

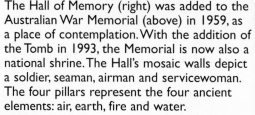

Australia's unknown soldier was originally buried in Adelaide Cemetery near Villers-Bretonneux in France, where the Australians, part of the British Expeditionary Force, had fought in 1918. After the Unknown's reburial in the Hall of Memory, a gravestone (inset) was placed in Adelaide Cemetery.

EUX (Somme) — Maisons en ruines. (Œuvre de la « ku tur » boche)
uses in ruins. Deed of the Hun (kultur) - A. P.

NEW ZEALAND

The Tomb of the Unknown Warrior
Te Toma O Te Toa Matangaro

NEW ZEALAND'S UNKNOWN WARRIOR began his long journey home in the 1920s, when plans for a Tomb of the Unknown Warrior were first made. On November 11, 2004, he was buried in his homeland.

The Tomb is built outdoors to give the public greater access to it. Designed by Kingsley Baird, it brings to mind the Southern Cross — a constellation visible all year round in New Zealand, and the inspiration behind the four five-pointed red stars on the country's flag. Light-grey marble crosses representing stars and soldiers are inlaid on the black granite Tomb. Around its base is a *karanga* (poem) in both Maori (the language of New Zealand's aboriginal people) and English, calling the Warrior's spirit back home:

The great pain we feel
Is for you who were our future.
Come back return home,
We have waited for you
Through the long years
You were away. Sorrow
Aches within me.

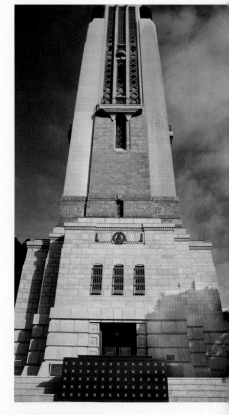

The dark stone of the Tomb is visible where it rests on the stairs leading to the entrance of the National War Memorial.

The gravestones of New Zealand's soldiers in France display a carving of a silver fern leaf (*ponga* in Maori), a national emblem. These two stones are marked *Known Unto God.*

The Tomb was blessed by a *kaumatua* (Maori elder) both before and after it was built. Four crosses/stars made of *pounamu,* a green stone prized by the Maori and associated with authority, status and peace, are inlaid on the lid.

AND ELSEWHERE . . .

"Monuments do not symbolize history, none of them. They all symbolize our relationship to that history." — *Harold Marcuse*

Memorials and monuments have been built around the world to honour those members of the armed forces who have fallen in battle throughout history, not just during the First World War. Also remembered are those civilians who have died because a war was waged. Some countries, such as Russia and France, have more than one memorial to unknown soldiers. Others, such as Switzerland, which have been neutral during times of war, have no national tombs for unknown soldiers.

Some nations have felt the need to have a place for remembrance, a place for regret, a place for quiet reflection, perhaps even peace.

Batalha Monastery in Portugal dates back to the 1300s. This old stereo card shows the inside of the beautiful Chapter House where "in a floor tomb, are enshrined Portugal's Unknown Soldiers; one from the French battlefields, and one from Africa to represent the colonial possessions. There are freshly cut flowers on the stone slab and beside it in war helmet a soldier is always on guard. In a tall iron lamp beside the tomb a flame burns unceasingly." The soldiers were buried in 1921. Today, two guards watch over the Tomb.

It's a long climb up to the Tomb of the Unknown Soldier in Belgrade, Serbia. Designed by famous Croatian-American sculptor Ivan Meštrović and completed in 1938, the building features eight granite sculptures of women representing different areas of the former Yugoslavia.

28

Unknown — No Longer

In 1916, Herbert Peterson, a twenty-one-year-old from Alberta, Canada, left his farm to enlist and fight in the First World War. Nearly fifty years later, seventeen-year-old Michael Blassie began his education at the United States Air Force Academy in Colorado, and served as a pilot during the Vietnam War. Both of these "brothers in arms" died serving their country. Identifying their remains many years later would have been impossible without key scientific advances.

Private Peterson's remains were found in 2003 when a gas pipeline was installed in a French housing subdivision just a few kilometres from Vimy Ridge. Uniform buttons identified the body as that of a Canadian soldier. Some authorities believed that he had been badly wounded and was being carried by another soldier when a nearby explosion killed them both and buried them in the earth. Three years of forensic investigation by historians, anthropologists, genealogists and scientists working together resulted in the identification of the soldier as Herbert Peterson.

Since 1936, Herbert Peterson's name has been inscribed on the Canadian National Vimy Memorial, along with the names of 11,285 other Canadian soldiers who were listed as "missing, presumed dead" in France. His name will remain there with those of his comrades.

DNA was the key. DNA, the genetic material found in most living cells, carries information that determines the characteristics we inherit from our parents. Samples taken from Private Peterson's nephew Herbert provided the needed proof that identified his uncle. Peterson became the first soldier, of the millions who fought in the Great War, to be identified using DNA samples from a living relative. In 2007, his family buried him among his comrades in France.

American president Ronald Reagan led a state funeral in 1984 for what *The New York Times* called "the only American known to have perished in the Vietnam War who is still unidentified." The war had been over for eleven years. A new crypt at the Tomb of the Unknowns in Washington had been excavated in 1973, but remained empty. By 1982, specialists had identified all the fallen Vietnam War service members except four. Three of those were later identified, or ruled out as perhaps not being Americans. Who was going to be buried in the waiting grave?

Pilot Michael Blassie's plane had been fired upon and had crashed in 1972. The crash site in Vietnam was located and some items and remains collected. An identification laboratory analyzed everything and thought they might be able to identify Michael Blassie. But in 1979 they decided that remains labelled as X-26 belonged to an Unknown. With great ceremony, the Vietnam War Unknown was buried between the Second World War and Korean War Unknowns in Washington, D.C.

But the Blassie family believed their son and brother had been mistakenly placed in the crypt. They collected evidence to prove their claim. People said that the government had rushed into selecting an Unknown.

DNA fingerprinting began to be used in forensic science and other cases in 1985, the year after the Vietnam Unknown's burial. Thirteen years later, Michael Blassie's remains were exhumed from the crypt. In a matter of weeks he was identified using DNA, and buried once again, with full military honours, in the Missouri cemetery where his father lay.

Officials decided that no attempts would be made to find another Unknown. Above the empty crypt where once the Vietnam War unknown soldier lay is this inscription: *Honoring and Keeping Faith with America's Missing Servicemen, 1958 – 1975.*

Thousands of POWs and MIAs, men and women from around the world, have disappeared in conflicts and peacekeeping missions since 1975. The search for these unknowns, each beloved and missed, continues.

On May 14, 1998, Michael Blassie's casket was removed from the crypt of the Vietnam War Unknown Soldier. A member of The Old Guard marches past the coffin before it is taken away for the tests that will prove the identity of the Unknown.

Herbert Peterson

Born: February 28, 1895 . . . .

Hometown: Berry Creek,
Alberta, Canada. . . . .

Member of: British Expeditionary
Force (infantry). . . . .

War: First World War . . . .

Former occupation: farmer . . . .

Rank: Private . . . .

Place of loss: near Vimy, France . . . .

Date of loss: June 9, 1917. . . . .

Presumed "Killed in Action/Body
not Recovered" . . . .

Age at death: 22. . . . .

Year of identification: 2007 . . . .

Years as unknown: 90 . . . .

Date of reburial: April 7, 2007. . . . .

Place of reburial: La Chaudière
Military Cemetery near Lens, France . . . .

Michael Joseph Blassie

April 4, 1948

Florissant, Missouri, USA

United States Air Force (pilot)

Vietnam War

student, U.S. Air Force Academy

1st Lieutenant

near An Loc, South Vietnam

May 11, 1972

Presumed "Killed in Action/Body not Recovered"

24

1998 (14 years as official U.S. Vietnam War Unknown Soldier)

26

July 11, 1998

Jefferson Barracks National Cemetery, St. Louis, Missouri, USA

Herbert Peterson's headstone is located at La Chaudière Cemetery in France. Canadian poppy pins were left by those who attended his burial, which was part of the events marking the rededication of the restored Vimy Memorial in 2007.

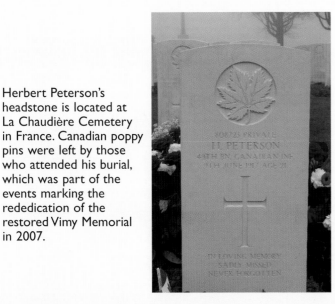

Flags and flowers adorn Michael Blassie's grave in St. Louis, Missouri. The back of the headstone lists the medals and decorations he was awarded, as well as these words: *Unknown Soldier/May 28, 1984/ May 14, 1998.*

31

Symbols Often Seen on Tombs and Gravestones

A symbol is something that represents something else — especially a material object used to represent something invisible.

Clockwise from upper left: eternal flame, dove, fruit, flowers, palm branch

Eternal flame: remembrance

Dove: peace

Fruit and flowers: life, nourishment of the soul, regeneration, resurrection

Palm branch: victory over death

Poppy: remembrance, eternal sleep

Torch: with flame, represents life, duty, immortality, truth, wisdom; without flame, represents death

Clockwise from upper left: lion, poppies, torch, urn, wreath

Lion: power, strength, war; also struggle, victory, courage and dignity. A lion guards the tomb against evil spirits. An old lion represents the setting sun; a young lion the rising sun.

IN MEMORY OF

Urn: the soul, immortality, final resting place

Wreath: victory

Others:

Broken Column: life cut short

Eagle: power, strength, war

Laurel/bay leaves: victory, triumph (often formed into a wreath)

Olive branch: peace, forgiveness, humanity

Reversed rifle: peace; mark of mourning and respect

Rose: victory, pride, love, purity

Sword: sheathed, represents temperance; inverted, may represent victory, giving up power or end of battle; broken, represents life cut short; crossed, represents life lost in battle

Willow tree: sorrow

SIGNIFICANT EVENTS

1914 – 1918 — • First World War (the Great War)

1919 — • Signing of the peace treaty, the Treaty of Versailles

1920 — • France dedicates *Le Tombeau du Soldat Inconnu*

1920 — • England buries its unknown warrior

1921 — • The United States buries its first unknown soldier

1921 — • Italy honours its Unknown in Rome

1922 — • Belgium inters its unknown soldier at the Congress Column

1925 — • Poland buries its unknown soldier at the Saxon Palace

1931 — • Germany honours its Great War Unknown at the *Neue Wache*

1932 — • Greece dedicates an empty tomb to "hold" all unknown Greek soldiers

1939 – 1945 — • Second World War

1959 — • Japan creates a pavilion especially for its unknown soldiers of the Second World War

1959 — • Iraq builds its Monument to the Unknown Soldier

1967 — • the Soviet Union honours its Second World War Unknown with a tomb near the Kremlin

1969 — • Germany buries two Unknowns

1982 — • Iraq's first monument is torn down and a new Monument to the Unknown Soldier is built

1993 — • Australia creates a special tomb for its unknown soldier at the Australian War Memorial

2000 — • Canada marks the millenium with the burial of its unknown soldier at the base of the National War Memorial in Ottawa

2004 — • New Zealand becomes the last of the Commonwealth countries to build a tomb for an unknown warrior

LEST WE FORGET

Soldier, rest! Thy warfare o'er,
Dream of fighting fields no more:
Sleep the sleep that knows not breaking,
Morn of toil, nor night of waking.

— *Sir Walter Scott*

Glossary

Armistice: an agreement between enemies to stop fighting; a truce

Casket/coffin: an oblong box in which a dead person is buried

Cenotaph: a monument erected in honour of a dead person or people who are buried elsewhere

Cenotaph (London)

Commonwealth War Graves Commission: a group that cares for the graves of British Commonwealth forces in cemeteries around the world

Cortège: a ceremonial, or funeral, procession

Crypt: an underground vault or chamber used as a burial place

Eulogy: a public speech sharing the achievements of a person who has died

Gun carriage: a wheeled vehicle used for moving a mounted gun; often used for carrying a coffin/casket in a funeral parade

MIA: a service member missing in action

Oculus: a circular or eye-shaped window

Plinth: a block or slab where a pedestal, column or statue is placed

POW: a service member taken by the enemy as a prisoner of war

Repatriation: to be brought back to the country of one's birth or citizenship

Sarcophagus: a stone coffin

Stereoscope: a viewer that makes two photographs of the same scene appear to be three-dimensional

Tomb: a chamber that holds a casket; a monument commemorating the dead

Oculus at *Neue Wache* (Berlin)

ACKNOWLEDGEMENTS

Heartfelt thanks are extended by the author to Scholastic Canada's Diane Kerner for her support, Andrea Casault for her design skills, and Sandy Bogart Johnston for her meticulous attention to detail and her commitment to our military history. Gratitude also goes to David Bennett of the Transatlantic Literary Agency Inc., Toronto; Lynne Sherren, John S. Brehaut and Janet Cox, Veterans Affairs Canada/Anciens Combattants Canada; Angus MacDermott, National Capital Commission, Canada; Manon Lévis, Rideau Hall, Ottawa; Leslie Carol Waggener, American Heritage Center, University of Wyoming; Jean-Francois Soyez and Lt. Bart Ghys, Belgian Defense Office; Katherine Hunt-Morr, Reuters; Susan Ross, Canadian War Museum; Jay Cossey; Liz Mills, *Legion Magazine;* Matt Barrett; Wilton S. Tifft; Jan and Doug Harper; Major Vassilios Anastasopoulos, Hellenic Army General Staff, Army History Directorate; Wanda M. Forsythe; Candia Lutyens, Lutyens Furniture Ltd.; Anne Letain; Irena Guzowska, Promotion Department, City of Warsaw; Wayne Ralph; SSG Christopher Gatrost, U.S. Army; Frank K. Pettit; Robert Crane; Kathryn Cole; Prof. Gary L. Catchen; Frank Shapleigh; Jamie Mackay, Ministry for Culture and Heritage, New Zealand; Mary-Ann Liu; Christine Reynolds, Westminster Abbey; National Archives & Records Administration, Maryland; Capt. Richard H. Asker, Ret.; Prof. Harold Marcuse, University of California/Santa Barbara; Prof. Ron Mellor; George Combs, Barrett Library, Alexandria, Virginia; Phillip Fraser, Australian War Museum; Peter Francis, Commonwealth War Graves Commission; Vasilios and Jim Samaras; Katie Simpson, *The Illustrated London News* Picture Library, Barbara Hehner; Herant Bablanian; Stella Partheniou Grasso; Andrei Leus; Koichi Takeshita; and finally, as ever, many thanks to Cal, Devon, and Brian Smiley for their loving support.

CREDITS

Grateful acknowledgement is made to all those who have granted permission to reprint copyrighted and personal material. Every reasonable effort has been made to locate the copyright holders for these images. The author and publisher would be pleased to receive information that would allow them to rectify any omissions in future printings.

Illustrative materials are from The Granfield Collection, except where noted.

Front cover: (inset) Frank Lucien Nicolet, *If ye break faith — we shall not sleep: BUY VICTORY BONDS* (detail; image altered), War Poster Collection, Rare Books and Special Collections Division, McGill University Library, WP1.B1.F1; (other images) The Granfield Collection

Back cover: (colour photo) courtesy of Cal Smiley; (black and white images) The Granfield Collection

Flag images: iStock

Title page: (centre) courtesy of Cal Smiley

Page 2: "Unknown," Linda Granfield

Page 5: (right) courtesy of Kathryn Cole

Page 6: courtesy of Cal Smiley

Page 7: (lower right) courtesy of Rideau Hall, Ottawa, Canada

Page 8: (upper left) Reuters; (upper right) Lynn Ball, *The Ottawa Citizen,* 227201; (lower right) *Tomb of the Unknown Soldier*, Photo: Harry Foster CMC, © Canadian War Museum (CWM)

Page 9: (left) courtesy of *Legion Magazine*, Dan Black; (lower right) courtesy of Cal Smiley

Page 13: (upper right) copyright Dean and Chapter of Westminster

Page 14: (centre) National Archives & Records Administration, Maryland, USA, 111-SC-104185

Page 15: (lower left) Richard Throssel Papers, American Heritage Center, University of Wyoming; (lower right) The United States Department of Defense, photo by U.S. Navy Cmdr. Jane Campbell

Page 16: (centre right) Jay Cossey/PhotographsFromNature.com; (lower right) courtesy of Cal Smiley

Page 17: (upper left) © Wilton S. Tifft; (lower left) © *The Illustrated London News* Picture Library; (far right) courtesy of Capt. Richard H. Asker, Ret.

Page 18: (lower right) courtesy of Jan and Doug Harper

Page 19: (right) courtesy of the Audiovisual Archive, Belgian Defense Office

Page 20: (all photos) courtesy of the Promotion Department, City of Warsaw, www.e-warsaw.pl

Page 21: (right) Prof. Harold Marcuse; (centre) courtesy of Brian L. Smiley

Page 22: (right) © Matt Barrett's Greece Travel Guide: www.greecetravel.com

Page 23: (lower left) Reuters

Page 24: (left) illustration by Colin Mayne; (centre) © Wilton S. Tifft; (right) © 2001, Frank K. Pettit

Page 25: (lower right) courtesy of SSG Christopher Gatrost, U.S. Army

Page 26: (left inset) © Robert Crane, www.ciaops.com; (lower right) Australian War Memorial, Negative Number PAIU2006/057.02

Page 27: (all photos) courtesy of the New Zealand Defence Force (NZDF)

Page 29: courtesy of Cal Smiley

Page 30: Reuters

Page 31: (upper left) courtesy of Veterans Affairs Canada, with permission of Mrs. Doreen Bargholz; (upper right) Reuters; (lower left) courtesy of Veterans Affairs Canada; (lower right) Reuters

Page 32: (right) courtesy of Jan and Doug Harper

Page 35: (lower) courtesy of Wanda M. Forsythe

Page 36: (right) courtesy of Brian L. Smiley

Quote on page 28: used with the permission of Prof. Harold Marcuse, Department of History, University of California, Santa Barbara, California.

INDEX

Alexandrovsky Gardens, 24

Allward, Walter, 7

Andrews, Mary Raymond Shipman, 16

Anderson, Grand Chief Howard, 8

Arc de Triomphe, 10, 11

Arlington National Cemetery, 14

Armistice, 3, 10

Baird, Kingsley, 27

Batalha Monastery, 28

Bean, Charles, 26

Bergamas, Maria, 18

Binyon, Laurence, 8

Blassie, Michael, 29, 31

Bonaparte, Napoleon, 10

Canada, 6–9, 7, 16, 29, 31

cemeteries, 4, 5, 6, 14, 18, 20, 23, 26, 31

Commonwealth War Graves Commission, 6

DNA (genetic identification), 5, 29, 30

eternal flame, 11, 17, 18, 21, 24, 32

First Nations, 8, 15

First World War (the Great War), 3, 4, 6, 7, 10, 12, 17, 18, 19, 20, 21, 22, 28, 29, 31

flowers, 5, 9, 11, 17, 18, 22, 23, 26, 28, 31, 32, 33

France, 6, 7, 8, 9, 10–11, 13, 14, 17, 26, 28, 29, 31

German Democratic Republic, 21

Great War, the, See First World War

guards, 9, 15, 17, 18, 20, 21, 22, 24, 28, 30

Haesebrouck, Raymond, 19

Hussein, Saddam, 25

Independence Day (Greece), 22

Iran-Iraq War, 25

Iraqi Army Day, 25

Kollwitz, Käthe, 21

Korean War, 4, 15

King George V, 12

Kremlin, 24

Lazaridis, Emmanuel, 22

Liu, Mary-Ann, 6,

Lutyens, Sir Edwin, 12

Maori, 27

Memorial Day, 15

Meštrović, Ivan, 28

Métivier, Paul, 8

National War Memorial, 7, 9

Pantheon, 10

Peace Tower, 7

Peloponnesian War, 22

Pericles, 22

Pershing, General John, 14

Peterson, Herbert, 29, 31

pilgrimages, 4, 17

Plenty Coups, Chief, 15

Polish-Soviet War, 20

Portugal, 28

poppy, 5, 16, 31, 33

prisoners of war (POWs), 30

Queen Elizabeth (Queen Mother), 17

Railton, David, 12

Reagan, Ronald, 30

Remembrance Day, 16

Royal Canadian Legion, 6

Royal Canadian Mounted Police, 8

Russia, 24, 28

Sarkozy, Nicolas, 11

Saxon Garden, 20

second Gulf War, 25

Second World War, 4, 8, 11, 15, 19, 20, 21, 23, 24

sentinels, See guards

Serbia, 28

Smith, Ernest, 8

Switzerland, 28

Syntagma Square, 22

Thin, Auguste, 10

Treloar, John, 26

Victor Emmanuel II, 18

Victoria Cross, 8, 13

Victory Day (National Unity Day/Italy), 18

Victory Day (Russia), 24

Vietnam War, 15, 29, 30, 31

Vimy Ridge/Memorial, 6, 7, 29, 31

Washington, D.C., 14, 15, 17, 30

Westminster Abbey 12, 13, 17

Wyatt, Brigadier-General L.J., 13

Yasukuni Shrine, 23

Younger, Sergeant Edward F., 14